Increasing Returns to Scale

INCREASING RETURNS TO SCALE

A SIMPLE WAY TO MAKE GOOD INVESTMENTS, AND NOT MAKE BAD INVESTMENTS, WHEN INVESTING IN COMPANY SHARES

BY

TIM WALSHAW

<publisher Tim Walshaw>

<2014>

Copyright © 2014 Tim Walshaw   All Rights Reserved.

All right reserved. No part of this publication may be reproduced, stored in a retrieval system, or transmitted, in any form or by any means, without the prior permission in writing of the publisher, nor be otherwise circulated in any form or binding or cover than that in which it is published and without a similar condition including this condition being imposed on the subsequent publisher.

ISBN: 978-0-9874946-5-8

FULL DISCLAIMER: THIS BOOK IS INTENDED SOLELY FOR INFORMATION PURPOSES AND IS NOT TO BE CONSTRUED, UNDER ANY CIRCUMSTANCES, BY IMPLICATION OR OTHERWISE, AS AN OFFER TO SELL OR A SOLICITATION TO BUY OR SELL OR TRADE IN ANY SECURITY. INFORMATION IS OBTAINED FROM SOURCES BELIEVED TO BE RELIABLE, BUT IS IN NO WAY GUARANTEED. NO GUARANTEE OF ANY KIND IS IMPLIED OR POSSIBLE WHERE PROJECTIONS OF FUTURE CONDITIONS ARE ATTEMPTED. IN NO EVENT SHOULD THE CONTENT OF THIS BOOK BE CONSTRUED AS AN EXPRESS OR IMPLIED PROMISE, GUARANTEE OR IMPLICATION BY OR FROM THE AUTHOR, PUBLISHER, EMPLOYEES, AFFILIATES OR OTHER AGENTS THAT YOU WILL PROFIT OR THAT LOSSES CAN OR WILL BE LIMITED IN ANY MANNER WHATSOEVER. SOME RECOMMENDED TRADES MAY INVOLVE SECURITIES HELD BY THE AUTHOR, AFFILIATES, EDITORS, WRITERS OR EMPLOYEES, AND INVESTMENT DECISIONS MAY BE INCONSISTENT WITH OR EVEN CONTRADICTORY TO THE DISCUSSION OR RECOMMENDATION IN THIS BOOK. PAST RESULTS ARE NO INDICATION OF FUTURE PERFORMANCE. SOME OF THE RESULTS DISCUSSED IN THE BOOK ARE A RESULT OF BACK-TESTING. ALL INVESTMENTS ARE SUBJECT TO RISK, WHICH SHOULD BE CONSIDERED PRIOR TO MAKING ANY INVESTMENT DECISIONS. CONSULT YOUR PERSONAL INVESTMENT ADVISERS BEFORE MAKING AN INVESTMENT DECISION. FOR PRIVACY PROTECTION, ABBREVIATED OR FICTITIOUS NAMES WERE USED FOR SOME OF THE INDIVIDUALS IN THIS BOOK. WHILE CERTAIN USERS OF THE RECOMMENDED TECHNIQUE HAD GREAT RESULTS, RESULTS ARE NOT THE SAME FOR EVERYONE.

CONTENTS

PREFACE		vi
INTRODUCTION		1
CHAPTER 1	EXPLANATION OF THE MEANING OF THE TERM 'RETURNS TO SCALE'	4
CHAPTER 2	THE RETURNS TO SCALE MODEL	8
CHAPTER 3	USING THE VALUE OF α AND β OF THE COBB DOUGLAS PRODUCTION MODEL FOR INVESTMENT DECISIONS	13
CHAPTER 4	SOURCING THE DATA, ANNUAL REPORTS, AND THE 10-K	16
CHAPTER 5	EXTRACTING FIGURES FOR INCOME Y, CAPITAL K, AND LABOR L FROM THE FINANCIAL STATEMENT	22
CHAPTER 6	ESTIMATING α AND β USING A SPREADSHEET	27
CHAPTER 7	THE SPREADSHEET RESULTS	31
CHAPTER 8	BUYING SHARES, MAINTAINING AND UPDATING YOUR PORTFOLIO	35
CHAPTER 9	DO SHARE PRICES ALWAYS INCREASE FOR INCREASING RETURNS TO SCALE COMPANIES?	40
CHAPTER 10	AVOIDING RUIN, OR AT LEAST THE HARMFUL EFFECTS OF A GENERAL SHARE CRASH!	42
CHAPTER 11	ON THE QUESTION OF FINDING SHARES TO INVEST IN, SHARE TIPS, DIVIDENDS, ASSORTED FURTHER ADVICE	45
CHAPTER 12	EXCURSIS, OR HOW COMPANIES CAN ACHIEVE INCREASING RETURNS TO SCALE, AND VALETE	50
CHAPTER 13	A MORE COMPLETE MATHEMATICAL EXPLANATION	55

PREFACE

This book offers you a very good way to invest profitably in good companies in the long term, and furthermore avoid losses by investing in bad ones. Its basic message is that if you invest in a company with increasing returns to scale, economic theory states that the company MUST be profitable; and furthermore, you are (almost) guaranteed an increased profit in the next period. If profits increase, share prices should also increase over the medium to long term. This is also a very simple method, not requiring complex methodology, or reliance on 'tips' or 'stories'. You can do it yourself over a few minutes each week.

Investing is a fearful business. You are liable to lose money. You may even have had experiences of losing money. Investing in shares is doubly fear ridden. Share prices go up and share prices go down. Investing in the short term is a zero sum game. That means you have a 50% chance of losing money!

True investing in the medium to long term can be a better proposition, if you invest in good companies and can get the timing right.

But what are good companies?

Most investors have had bitter experience of advice from advisers/stockbrokers selling them 'duds', 'dogs', whatever. Yet you are dependent on this advice. Few have the time and resources to research in depth to find good investments. At best you read the papers, troll the internet, and get 'tips' which not only prove worthless, but you suspect these shares are being pushed by the internet site so someone else can sell out. The odds are lined up against the small investor; also indeed the medium sized investor with a fund worth a few million dollars but who cannot afford to employ a full time researcher, even if you could find someone sufficiently brilliant.

So you put the money in a Fund, with 2 1/2% commission, good one year, and lousy for several years.

This book offers a way out. You can do this simple investment research work yourself. The work, yes there is work involved, will take a few minutes maintenance each week, and for most people, is enjoyable. And you will be ahead of the crowd, at least until this method takes off. The method will, admittedly after a time consuming first stage, (I suggest a week away in a cabin in the woods), will provide you with a list of company shares which are well worth investing in, and a suggested division of your investment portfolio for each of your chosen shares. Most importantly the methodology will weed out the 'dogs', (often highly touted investments), which if avoided will immeasurably improve your investment portfolio.

What is this magic method? It is a simple technique drawn from the theory of Economics, called 'Returns to Scale'. Your aim is to invest in firms with Increasing Returns to Scale, and avoid investing in firms with Decreasing Returns to Scale, or worse still (and there are too many of these) Negative Returns to Scale.

And yes, year after year, share prices of companies which remain on increasing returns to scale keep increasing, good times and bad, while the other share prices peak and fall. Why? Simple. Those companies on increasing returns to scale MUST (as required by economic theory) be always profitable. And their profits MUST (as required by economic theory) keep increasing as long as the firm remains on increasing returns to scale.

There, that is a piece of useful economic knowledge for you!

But WHY am I writing this book? To make a few dollars selling it? No. In the hope of gaining commissions for investment advice. No. After reading this book, you can do the investment yourself. You don't need my advice. Anyway, I don't need these commissions.

The reason I am writing the book is to improve the world.

Yes, if enough investors use this technique, the world will be a better place. What? How? It is acknowledged among economists that if most firms operated under increasing returns to scale; not on average, as at present, constant returns to scale; economic growth will be faster, unemployment will be lower, average wealth and income will be higher, and the economy will operate more efficiently. To put it simply, it would be a better world.

Now if it becomes a standard investment guideline that a firm must operate under increasing returns to scale if people and funds are to invest in that firm's shares, every firm will take good care to operate under increasing returns to scale always. Irrational investment decisions will be curbed, the superfluous hiring of staff will be discouraged, excessively exuberant management decisions will be opposed, and constant attention will be paid, not to the vague concept of the 'bottom line', but to remain within the tight guidelines for increasing returns to scale.

So I hope that when this technique becomes prevalent, a better world will be ushered in.

But in the meantime, investors are resistant to change. The first users of this book will make substantial profits at the expense of the ignorant and stupid. After all, you will be among the first to find those good investments, and someone must buy at a reasonable price those dud shares you are selling. However you will need to do a small amount of work to work out the returns to scale for each firm that you are interested in. But if you do apply yourself to this technique I don't need to wish you good fortune. Fortune will find you.

INTRODUCTION

Before I start on the subject of this short book, I believe it is necessary to say just a little about myself, and why I came to write this book.

I am a university graduate in economics and an economist by trade. And by trade, I mean a very practical economist, who through his professional lifetime has used his knowledge to advance the economic welfare (all right, wealth, but economist love using these high sounding terms) of first his employers and then his clients. I started my professional life as an economist in a government economic research organization, but I found that a government research organization was an oxymoron, and went out on my own. I started in international consultancy, and then followed the money trail to investment and financial advice, and prospered.

Why did I prosper? I used my knowledge of economics, and economic theory, to vastly improve the quality of investment advice. Most investment advice is bad, and loses clients money. I began by providing macro advice, that is advice on the outlook of the economy, and I was better than 8 out of 10 economists proffering this advice. But I moved into microeconomic advice, that is advice on individual firms; how they were structured, how they performed. And yes, my advice was vastly better and more profitable than advice given by other company analysts.

Why? Not because I claim to be cleverer, though I admit that in the vast majority of cases I was. No, it was because the current investment advice methodology is fundamentally flawed. It falls into two categories. "stories", (including the illegal insider sort), and "accounting ratios".

You have all seen investment 'stories'. Your stockbroker sends them incessantly. If you are a fund manager you get a stack of them every day, often from your own inside analysts. "Such and such a mine has found a new deposit. Such a company has been given a big contract. The economy is picking up, and consumers like x company cars." If you rush out and buy (or occasionally sell) on the basis of these stories, and if the stories always work, you would be a millionaire in no time at all. Older and wiser investors know that the vast majority of these stories fall flat. They never seem to resolve into higher long-term profits. I call these stories 'tips', and they are less valuable than on the racetrack. At least on the track there are only a small number of horses in each race. On the stock market there are myriads of share issues.

Accounting ratios. They often come with the stories. It is an attempt to appear 'scientific'. The liquidity ratio is such and such, and the quick ratio is such and such. Accountants (there are too many of them in investment) have taken over the investment advice industry, and they use these ratios non-stop. Yes, these ratios can often be useful, especially if a company is in a bad way. Most companies attempt to keep their ratios in acceptable bounds. If they are unable to do this, this is an obvious sign that the company is in trouble. Ratio analysis can prevent you making a bad investment, and thus losing your money. But making more money? I have yet to see any example where investing in a company with 'good' ratios makes money. "They have a good liquidity ratio, therefore I must invest." Warren Buffett claims to do this, but I am pretty sure his investigations go much deeper than that.

Furthermore, from an economic point of view, averages and ratios are nonsense, as everything happens at the 'margin'. But marginal analysis is difficult, usually requiring economic models, expertise and the use of computers. Even if most investment analysts knew how to do marginal analysis, most investors would not understand the result. The method I propose is a simplified method of marginal analysis, and yes, it uses a simplified economic model.

Yes, I do have issues with accountants and accounting rules. Briefly because you cannot trust the published profits, among a lot of other things. Between double entry bookkeeping and the published figures a lot of nasty things happen. For instance, profit figures are adjusted upwards in the accounting process by increases in capital values. Also in my opinion accrual accounting is a recipe for deceit, as used by Enron. As an economist I take strong exception to this. For my clients, I calculate the 'real' profits, the "economic rents" of a company. I have a nifty way of doing this. But that is a story for another day.

This book is about a quick, easy and highly effective method of finding the true state of a company. How efficient it is. And how prosperous it is in terms of its income. This method gives three figures which measure how efficiently the firm is operating: - how efficient its labor is, how efficient is its use of capital, and most importantly how efficient the company as a whole is. In effect it is a measure of the efficiency and competence of the company management. As a secondary outcome, it is an effective measure of the size and trend of company revenue, and the company's market situation. This information cannot be hidden or manipulated by accounting devices.

What this recommended methodology cannot do is to tell the future, whether good or bad. But if you invest in the best type of companies you find using the economic technique I recommend, if the company income falls due to some unexpected external event, the company will not suffer to a great extent, or to the degree of its less efficient competitors. I have also found that this measure can be used as a measure of "good management". The best companies chosen by this method will take every advantage of the prevailing economic conditions, and continues to prosper in good and bad years.

So what is this measure? The economic term is RETURNS TO SCALE. For non-economists I shall briefly describe the concept in the next chapter. I recommend investing in companies with INCREASING RETURNS TO SCALE, and avoiding firms with CONSTANT and DECREASING RETURNS TO SCALE, and especially avoiding investing in firms with NEGATIVE RETURNS TO SCALE.

CHAPTER 1

EXPLANATION OF THE MEANING OF THE TERM RETURNS TO SCALE

The Returns to Scale concept relates outputs of a firm to inputs to a firm. Not necessarily inputs to a manufacturing process. The firm may be purely a service firm, such as Google, where the only inputs are capital equipment (computers), employee effort, a bit of electricity and paper.

The measure of returns to scale is related to *proportional changes*, not the actual quantities. This obviated the problem which bedeviled economists for centuries – how to relate apples to oranges, and is monetary value a suitable substitute?

Scale is defined as the total quantity of all the inputs used by the firms in a given time. The greater quantity of inputs used, the greater the scale.

Returns is the measure of the total quantity of output created by the firm using these inputs. A suitable measure for returns is revenue or income. (Note – Returns are NOT profits).

If the *proportional change* of output is the same *proportional change* of the inputs, then the firm is said to be operating under **constant returns to scale**.

If *proportional change* of output is less than the *proportional change* of the inputs, then the firm is said to be operating under **decreasing returns to scale**.

If *proportional change* of output is greater than the *proportional change* of the inputs, then the firm is said to be operating under **increasing returns to scale**.

An illustrative diagram is shown in Figure 1. In this diagram, 'returns' are in effect the revenue of the firm. If returns increase at a faster rate than scale, that is accelerate, the slope gets steeper. This is the area of increasing returns to scale.

Similarly, if returns decrease at a faster rate than the rate of increase of scale, that is decelerate, the slope gets shallower. This is the area of decreasing returns to scale.

In between there is a brief period when the slope equals one (the slope is forty five degrees). Neither acceleration nor deceleration occurs, as the returns increase at the same rate as scale. This happens even though the total returns are still increasing. This is the point of constant returns to scale.

Economic purists will argue that this diagram should be drawn in terms of the positions of isoquant curves. But this book is not an economics textbook, but is aimed at non-economists trying to get an insight into a new method to analyze investments. In this diagram economic purity has been sacrificed to practicality.

There is an additional reason why I used this diagram. Economists generally ignore a very important area of economic activity – **negative returns to scale**. Isoquant diagrams assume rising returns always as scale increases. Yet as can be seen from the diagram, returns can fall as scale increases. This outcome may be a surprise to most economists, who assume an always-functioning efficiently running economy. But a high proportion of firms operate under negative returns to scale. That is, as scale increases, returns fall. This is a really shocking revelation. This was especially true in the US and Europe after the 2008 financial crisis. In actual practice, as you will discover, a surprisingly high proportion of the firms operating in the free market economies operate, at least for a while, within this Soviet style arrangement. As more resources are poured into them, revenue starts falling, and the less profitable they become. If nothing else, this book will help readers avoid this type of firm when investing, so that they don't drop their money into what is effectively an investment black hole.

For those who do not understand the meaning of 'Returns to Scale' from the brief description above I recommend that you search on the internet for a suitable exposition of Returns to Scale on Google and YouTube, or some other site. I am sure there will be a clear description in the internet that will help you.

Now a reader may have an additional question itching in his mind. Why, if as this book claims, estimating increasing and decreasing returns to scale so easy, and so useful, why is not its use already universal? The answer is that for ideological (Marxist) reasons in the first half of the twentieth century, economist proved "mathematically" that while constant returns to scale was possible, both increasing and decreasing returns to scale were not. According to the Palgrave Dictionary of Economics, as described by the economist John Eatwell, the economist Piero Sraffa "demonstrated that *neither* increasing or *decreasing* returns to scale are compatible with the assumption of perfect competition or of partial–equilibrium supply curves." Given Sraffa's influence at the time, this put a fence around the subject. Sraffa's reputation has subsequently taken a beating, and his ideas such as "re-switching" have been falsified. While it is true that the concept of perfect competition necessarily assumes constant returns to scale, and so does input output theory and general equilibrium, these were enthusiasms of academic economists in the twentieth century. No economics teacher nowadays gives Sraffa's ideas more than passing mention in the history of economic thought. The Sraffan-Eatwell reservations on increasing/decreasing returns to scale have been demolished by James Buchanan (a Nobel Prize winning economist) and others.

A glance at the diagram at the end of this chapter shows that increasing and decreasing returns to scale do and must exist. A knowledge of how to calculate their value can be profitably used.

Figure 1

RETURNS TO SCALE

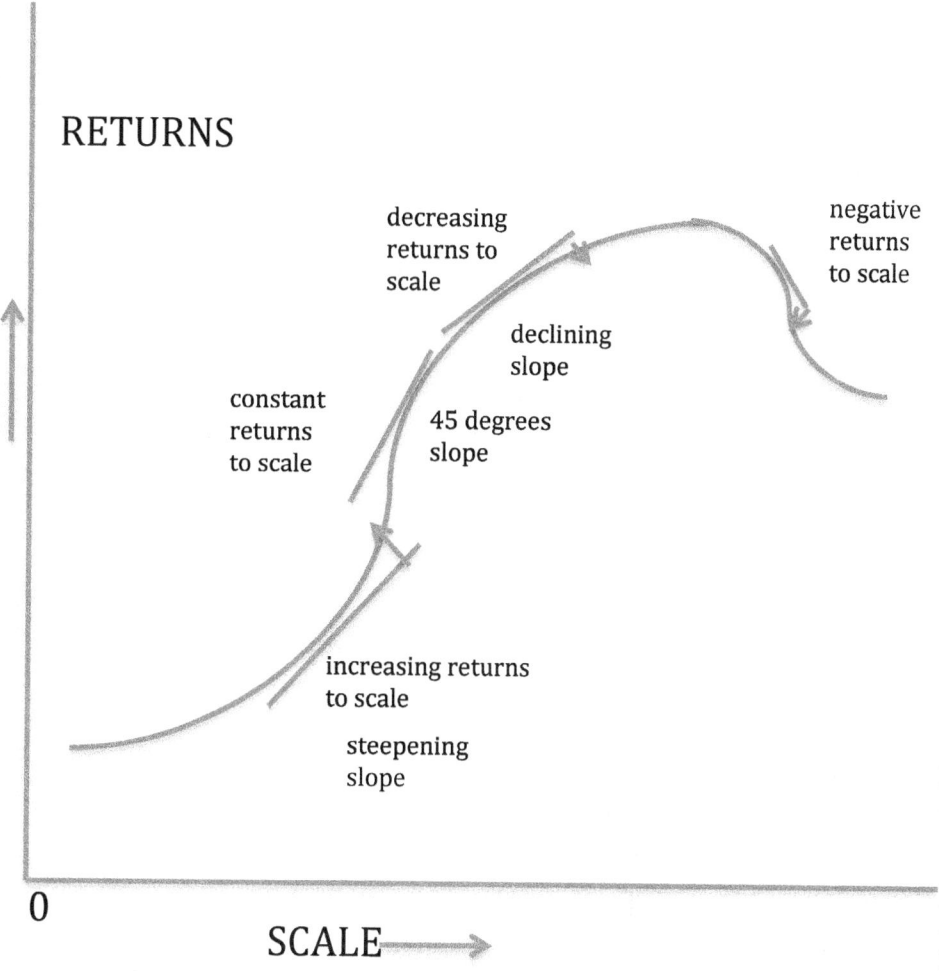

CHAPTER TWO

THE RETURNS TO SCALE MODEL

This section descends into economic speak. The reason why I included this section is that many people, since they are investing their money on my advice in this book, need reassurance that I didn't pluck a wild idea from the air and proceed to use it, but the process is based on correct economic theory.

Thus I describe how the process will estimate the returns to scale of a firm, if you follow the instructions of the book. I intend to demonstrate that the methodology, from the point of view of economic theory, is correct.

Economists work with 'models', mathematical formulae based on economic theory, which are supposed to explain the workings of that area of the economic system, and hopefully, when you put numbers in them, produce interesting and useful answers and forecasts.

Over time economists have attempted, with greater and lesser success, to measure business activity with a wide variety of models. They have usually attempted to relate 'outputs' to 'inputs', with the general aim of measuring the behavior of business and other interesting variables such as efficiency.

Two of the most traditional inputs used, and the simplest, were measures of labor and capital. Models of this type are called 'production functions'. A wide variety of production functions are used by economists, but one, created by the economist Charles Cobb and the mathematician Paul Douglas, in 1927, is one of the simplest, and indeed is the one most often used for that reason. This is the Cobb Douglas Production Function.

Cobb hypothesized that most industry at the time was operating under Constant Returns to Scale, and wanted a model to confirm this. After advice from Paul Douglas, he came up with the model

$$Y = AK^{\alpha}L^{\beta}$$

Where Y is the value of total production (a proxy being the value of total sales revenue)

K is the amount of capital input (a proxy can be the value of total assets)

L is the labor input (a proxy can be labor cost)

α is the elasticity of income with respect to capital. Thus $\alpha = 0.45$, an increase in capital costs of \$1 will increase revenue by 45 cents

β is the elasticity of income with respect to labor. Thus if $\beta = 0.45$, an increase in labor costs of \$1 will increase income by 45 cents.

Under constant returns to scale, $\alpha + \beta = 1$. This is the constraint imposed on the model so that it operates under constant returns to scale. (Have a chat with a mathematician if you don't believe it).

A is called Total Factor Productivity. In fact it is a scalar adjustment factor, adjusting the scale of Y to the scales of L and K to make $\alpha + \beta = 1$.

So much for theory. But it can be seen that the imposition of the constraint $\alpha + \beta = 1$ hamstrung the search for increasing returns to scale using the Cobb Douglas Production Function.

Nevertheless I decided to use it for its inherent simplicity. As such a smaller data set can be used. Just two succeeding years.

One method to loosen the constraint is to include a constant c, (c.f. see the Wikipedia entry on 'Returns to Scale') which is also influenced by the factors α and β. Multiplying both variables by c,

$$Y = A(cK)^{\alpha}(cL)^{\beta}$$

$$= Ac^{\alpha}c^{\beta}K^{\alpha}L^{\beta}$$

Now for simplicity's sake, $Ac^{\alpha}c^{\beta}$ can be called a variable D.

Thus $Y = DK^{\alpha}L^{\beta}$

I use a two period model as that provides the minimum amount of data needed for this model.

We assume that α and β are the same over two successive years. We can do this as the operational structure of a firm is likely to change slowly.

$Y_1 = D_1 K_1^{\alpha} L_1^{\beta}$

$Y_2 = D_2 K_2^{\alpha} L_2^{\beta}$

Where Y_1 is Revenue in year 1

Y_2 is Revenue in year 2

K_1 is Capital in year 1

K_2 is Capital in year 2

L_1 is Labor cost in year 1

L_2 is Labor cost in year 2

And D_1 and D_2 are the coefficients in year 1 and year 2.

Now, as explained before, returns to scale are measured as proportional changes.

The usual method to deal with this is to convert these formulae into a logarithmic format, which can be used to denote proportional changes. This has the additional benefit of simplifying the model by converting it into additive form, and make it more tractable.

Thus

$Ln Y_1 = \alpha \ln K_1 + \beta \ln L_1 + \ln D_1$

$Ln Y_2 = \alpha \ln K_2 + \beta \ln L_2 + \ln D_2$

The term ln is the denotation of the exponential form of the logarithm. You can also use logs to the base 10 and others. It does not make any difference in practice, but exponential ln is a bit more convenient to use.

It is further assumed that $\ln D_1 - \ln D_2 = 0$, as the operational structure of a firm is likely to change slowly.

These formulae become after some mathematical manipulation (if you want the complete mathematical explanation turn to Chapter 13)

$$\beta = \frac{\ln Y_1 - \alpha \ln K_1}{\ln L_1} \text{ or } \frac{\ln Y_2 - \alpha \ln K_2}{\ln L_2}$$

Experiment will show that that the values of both formulae are usually very close.

Thus, reworking the above two formulae,

$$\alpha = \frac{\ln L_2 \ln Y_1 - \ln L_1 \ln Y_2}{\ln L_2 \ln K_1 - \ln L_1 \ln K_2}$$

You have got the values of α and β!

α is the measure of the relative efficiency of capital for the firm. β is the measure of the relative efficiency of labor for the firm.

The top formula estimates the value of α using the known values of Y_1, K_1, L_1, Y_2, K_2, L_2. That is, the values for income, capital and labor for two successive years.

To estimate β substitute the value of α into one of the above formulas for β. Either formula will give a very close result.

Now for the value of Returns to Scale, the final formula is very simple.

If R is the value of Returns to Scale for the firm.

$$R = \alpha + \beta$$

So there you are. A theoretically correct method (allowing for simplifying assumptions) for estimating α and β, and thus Returns to Scale!

The Golden Formulae!

So much for theory. For those of more practical bent, and only interested in how this concept will help you make money on the stock market, the next chapters describe how you can in practice use the above formulas to estimate what returns to scale their proposed investment operates under. Together with a figure for the efficiencies of each of labor and capital – a very interesting result.

These formulae are of course very easy to apply to spreadsheets.

CHAPTER THREE

USING THE VALUE OF α AND β OF THE COBB DOUGLAS PRODUCTION MODEL FOR INVESTMENT DECISIONS

Total company returns to scale

With this formulation,

If α + β > 1 (positive) the firm has increasing returns to scale

If α + β = 1 the firm has constant returns to scale.

If 0 < α + β < 1 the firm has decreasing returns to scale.

However firms can have α + β < 0 (negative returns to scale). Firms with negative returns to scale are on the downward slope of the expenditure/revenue curve. (See Figure 1). A large number of firms are in this situation. Increased expenditure on capital or labor actually <u>reduces</u> revenue!

The higher the absolute figure α + β the higher the rate of decreasing or increasing returns to scale.

The relative efficiency of capital α and labor β

If α > 0, the revenue elasticity for capital expenditure is positive. The value of α means that for every additional dollar invested in capital, revenue increases by the same number of dollars. So for example if α = 2.5, increased expenditure of one dollar on capital would increase revenue 2.5 dollars.

If α < 0, the revenue elasticity of capital expenditure is negative. The value of -α means that for every additional dollar invested in capital, revenue decreases the same number of dollars. If α = -2.5, increased expenditure on capital of one dollar would decrease revenue by 2.5 dollars.

If β > 0, the revenue elasticity for expenditure on labor is positive. The value of β means that for every additional dollar spent on labor, revenue increases by the same number of dollars. So for example if β = 2.5, increased expenditure of one dollar on labor would increase revenue 2.5 dollars.

If β < 0, the revenue elasticity for expenditure on labor is negative. The value –β means that for every additional dollar spent on labor, revenue decreases by the same number of dollars. . If β = -2.5, increased expenditure on labor of one dollar would decrease revenue by 2.5 dollars

And of course vice versa. Reducing labor costs when β is negative increases profits.

However when β is positive reducing labor costs reduces profits! So when some idiot bean counter says it 'saves money' to reduce labor costs, don't do it if β is positive! You are destroying your source of increased profits!

As an added bonus the estimated value, α + β, would show the <u>degree</u> of increasing or decreasing returns to scale. So you could make scalar comparisons between firms.

What is more interesting from the investment point of view are negative results for α + β. Negative returns for α + β means negative returns to scale. Increased resource inputs leading to falling revenue. This is a Soviet economy result, yet it is very common. Only a very stupid investor would knowingly invest in this type of company.

The suggested investment methodology you should use is as follows:

1. Estimate α and β for the firm in question.
2. Add α + β to obtain the returns to scale.
3. If α + β is negative reject investing in this company.
4. If either α or β is negative, but α + β is positive, carefully investigate the management of this company. Why is its increasing returns to scale dependent on only one factor, efficient capital use or efficient labor use? Is this likely to change?
5. If α + β is greater than one and has a high positive value compared to other companies, and both α and β are positive, seriously investigate whether to invest. If α + β is greater than one, this

means the company has increasing returns to scale. It is potentially profitable in almost any circumstances. (Theoretically a firm with increasing returns to scale <u>must</u> be profitable). Look at its price, p/e ratio, the market situation and the general state of the economy and the industry before investing. However a high positive α + β value is a very good positive indicator for a positive investment decision, unless the share is vastly over valued.

This is a very simple methodology, and can be very easily applied to a large number of companies at a time for comparison purposes. Use a spreadsheet!

CHAPTER FOUR

SOURCING THE DATA, ANNUAL REPORTS AND THE 10-K

The next two chapters cover two aspects of the same subject. This chapter is the vexed topic of actually finding the company financial reports/statements. The following chapter covers extracting the figures for Income Y, Capital K, and Labor L from those financial statements.

No, Virginia, companies just don't hand you the Financial Statements on a plate. "Oh, they are just in the Annual Reports!" Finding a Financial Statement is, for most companies, made hard and difficult. Only a few small companies with good profits make their financial statements easy to find. If you employ someone to find the company financial statements, give them a piece of leather to put between their teeth and double their salaries. If you find someone who does the job of finding financial statements rapidly and well, they are worth their weight in gold!

Financial Reports/Statements are usually located towards the end of the Company Annual Reports. You need to find the latest Annual Report of that company.

In many countries, such as the US, Quarterly Reports are published. As a source of financial information these reports suffer for three reasons:
1. They are not audited, thus they are likely to be inaccurate (a lot more than the audited reports).
2. In many cases the figures reported are erratic and unstable. This could be because of the above-mentioned cause of inaccuracy of the report, or seasonal effects.
3. In many cases, useful figures for labor costs are not published in these reports. Accurate and consistent labor-cost figures are essential for this method.

Private aggregators

I am aware of the existence of private aggregators and providers of company information, who can more easily provide the Annual Report information required. These sources are used by large funds and investors. If you have access to this information, lucky you. In particular, these private sources often provide employee numbers and wage costs for the companies reported on. This wage cost information is not generally available from Annual Reports in most countries. However these aggregator services are expensive. Unless you are very wealthy or run a large investment fund, it is unlikely that you can afford these aggregator services, and I am writing this book to explain how even a small investor can improve their investment performance.

ACCESSING FINANCIAL REPORTS

So you don't have access to the proprietary data sets (I won't name them, but most are very good), and you need to go directly to the source, the Annual Reports.

Nowadays, these Annual Reports are available on the internet, on the company web sites. But often the Annual Reports can be found on the company web site only with a great deal of difficulty, as they are well hidden. I have found that as a general rule, if the company has problems, - financial, management, cultural, - a number of obstructions are placed in front of you to prevent you accessing any useful financial results.

SEC Reports – the EDGAR site and the 10-K

However in the US, listed companies are required to file and publish a very useful annual financial reporting form with the Securities Exchange Commission (SEC), the 10-K. This information can be found on the SEC web site, called EDGAR, though the same information and form is sometimes also published on the company web site. The 10-K contains the Annual Financial Report, usually in a standard format together with a massive amount of detailed operational information. Even so, some firms, deliberately I think, try to make it difficult to access financial information even from this source. Be warned. In over 90% of these cases I have found, where you have access problems, the company is what I call 'dodgy'. Your eventual Returns to Scale figures, obtained after much persistence, will confirm this. So it is dangerous to give up!

So, how does one find the 10-K? Type in to your search engine SEC EDGAR. The page you find is one of several SEC web sites that allow you to search for a particular company.

Type in the company name (not the stock exchange code) into the search box near the top of the page, and press 'enter'. The search engine comes up with a list of similar sounding companies. (There are many, many, companies in the investment galaxy, and while having identical names is forbidden, similar sounding names are allowed.) Choose the company you think it is and double click.

You get another list. Dozens, even hundreds of cryptic titles, 4-Q, 4-K, 8-K, many others. You would think American companies have nothing better to do except file reports with the SEC! They are filed in date order, the most recent first. Anyway, look for 10-K.

If you can't find 10-K, and you often can't, there is another search box at the top. Type in 10-K and enter.

You now get a reduced list, most of which are 10-K's. Select the one at the top, which is the most recent, and double click that.

You then get the standard SEC title page with the name of the company. Scroll down to the index page, which is the next page or two. You will immediately see that the SEC report is massive. Most of that stuff is of limited use to you, unless you are 1. An expert in company law. 2. You know what you are looking for. 3. You have invested in the company and suspect the company directors of malfeasance, or you think something strange is going on. The "risks" pages are always interesting, and are good for a laugh if nothing else. No, to be serious, the company is covering itself for EVERYTHING, and can claim "YOU HAVE BEEN INFORMED AND WARNED".

An alternative search method to going directly to the SEC web site is to Google the company name and 10-K. This often takes you directly there.

Go down the SEC report index, and down near the end you get "Section 8,……Page….. Financial Statement"

Scroll down to that page. Down, down, past all the list of options the directors have awarded themselves, and the antics they get up to.

The Financial Statement is quite brief, and is in turn divided in three sections.

1. Revenue (The Income Statement).
2. The Balance Sheet.
3. The Cash Flow Statement.

Ignore the Cash Flow Statement for now. I shall write another book on how to get interesting goodies from that.

The financial statements are usually highlighted in blue in the 10-K form, but are not otherwise very long. You get a few figures from both the Revenue Statement and the Balance Sheet, as will be shown in the next chapter.

Company Annual Reports

The alternative method (especially if the company is not quoted in the US) is to access Annual Reports from the company web site. (There are special SEC report forms for foreign companies quoted in the US, the 20-K and the 20-F. It is still more worthwhile to look at these than the foreign company Annual Reports, which can be quite peculiar).

Publicly quoted companies must publish their own Annual Reports each year, which they usually publish on their company web site. This is very much a public relations exercise, and sometimes the actual financial statements are well hidden.

Indeed some offending companies fail to publish important figures in their financial statements. They give the "Net Revenue" at the top of the Revenue page, not the "Total Revenue" figure; give summaries which hide expenses in "Total Expenses" and so on. If this happens look in the SEC report, which requires obligatory figures; or from my wide experience, I suggest giving these companies a wide berth. There is plenty more fish in the sea. Do not invest in firms with incomplete financials.

Exercise in finding a Company Financial Report/Statement

As already discussed, finding a company financial report/statement is not easy. Actually it can be a real pain. You need a lot of experience to track them down quickly.

I suggest that from here on, as an exercise, that you open a company web site, and refer to it as I go through the method. Any company. General Electric for example.

Look up General Electric on Google and find their home web page. Look on the top right hand corner of the 'ribbon' at the top and for a small address "Investor services". (As I said, this not going to be easy). Investor services is also full of public relations stuff, but if you hunt around you can find a reference to Annual Reports. (No you don't want Quarterly Reports – remember what I said – they are un-audited and full of guff). Find the latest year's Annual Report and open it,

So you have found the latest company Annual Report web site. You are still not there by a country mile. The Annual Report will be really gee wiz, and try to impress you, or try to sell you stuff. But tucked away in a tiny corner is the address of the location of the company Financial Statement. It is up to you to find it. Don't worry, after a time you will become quite expert at squirreling it out. But for a beginner it can be frustrating. But it must be there. It is a legal requirement nowadays for all companies to place the Financial Statement on its web site. (But not make it easy to access. Some very well known companies seem to go out of their way to make it all but impossible to view their financial results. As I have said frequently, don't invest in such companies).

So it is worth repeating the process.

So Step 1. Look at the company home page. Look for a 'ribbon' giving the list of additional pages of the web site. This ribbon is usually at the top of the opening page, but various recalcitrant companies try to hide it at the bottom, and you have to scroll down to find it.

Remember what I said. The more difficult a company makes it to find their Financial Statement, the more likely they are to be in trouble. The combination of dishonesty and stupidity cannot be gainsaid. But nevertheless it is worth persisting to confirm this.

Step 2. In this ribbon you usually see a heading 'Investor information', 'investor', or such like, or this heading can be hidden under a heading 'Company Information'.

Step 3. Open this investor page. You are not there yet. You now get a whole list of reports and other publications. Most of these are useless for our purpose. Look for 'Annual Reports', or better still 'Annual Report year such and such' – then choose the Annual Report with the latest year.

Some of these other reports are Quarterly Reports. Ignore those. But if you get Report 10-K (latest year) that is pure gold. Open that. It contains a massive amount of detailed information about what the Directors are up to, but scroll down towards (see the section above) the end when you get to two pages – Revenue, and Balance Sheet. That's all you need,

Step 4. Many poor punters just get a web page of the Annual Report, or an Adobe pdf, or some complicated site that makes it very difficult to navigate – a warning sign already discussed. OK, ignore the bright pictures and try to find the index. This should give the page in the Annual Report at which the Financial Statement is situated. Invariably it is near the end of the Annual Report. Scroll down to this page.

Step 5. First open the Revenue Statement, which is usually first, to find Income Y AND Labor L, and then move to the next page, the Balance Sheet, the find Capital K.

But as I said, if the company is American, the best bet is to go directly to the SEC 10-K. The financial report is not hidden, and it is in a standard format.

How to obtain each set of accounting information is described in detail in the forthcoming chapter.

CHAPTER FIVE

EXTRACTING THE FIGURES FOR INCOME Y, CAPITAL K, AND LABOR L FROM THE FINANCIAL STATEMENT

All Financial Statements have a standard format. Once you know this, it is easy to extract the required information (if it is published).

First prepare the form described below for writing down the financial figures that you obtain.

GENERAL ELECTRIC

	Y Income	K capital	L Labor
Year 1	147288	718189	54185
Year 2	147359	685328	53912

The table is headed by the company name, in this case General Electric.

It is a table of three rows and four columns. The second and third rows are titled Year 1 and Year 2, as shown above. The second, third and fourth column are headed in turn, Y Income, K Capital, and L Labor.

Now there is an important aspect about the figures. The amounts in this case are in millions of dollars. It is important not to vary the scale, which could be having millions in one column and hundreds of thousands in another. Therefore I recommend that you use the same scale as you find in the accounts. If the accounts give their totals in millions, use millions. If the accounts give their totals in thousands, use thousands. What you must NOT do is use millions in one set of figures, say assets, and thousands in another set of figures, say labor. As these figures are interconnected in the formulae, this will throw the calculations out. Remember this.

On a related issue, some companies publish the number of persons employed. Should you use this figure instead of the published labor costs? The answer is NO. To put it simply, mixing apples and oranges will throw the calculations out. All the figures will have to be in dollars.

Use the same scale of thousands or millions of dollars as published. I say again, the formula is so constructed that changing scales for one accounting type will throw the results out.

Use the same scale and dollar figures throughout.

Income Y

Go to the Revenue Statement, which is usually located first.

Now what is Income Y? We are looking for what economists call suitable proxies. For company income, I use the accounting figure **Total Revenue**. This is the total sales of the company plus income from other sources such as investments.

Total Revenue is generally found on the top line on the income statement. (Certain companies only publish Net Revenue figures, not Total Revenue. That is better than nothing. As discussed with the Labor figures, if the ratio of the amount deducted remains the same in both years, a major inaccuracy is not introduced. You are looking at proportional changes between years.). Certain companies give a breakdown of the Total Revenue figure. Always go for the Total Revenue or failing that the Net Revenue figure in order to obtain Y. Accounting rules on this measure are strict and for once do not favor the company. This is the easiest figure of the three to find.

Finding Y_1 and Y_2. Two succeeding years income. You will invariably find these figures next to each other in different columns in the Revenue Statement. But be aware. In most financial statements the most recent year is the LEFT HAND column. For those unfamiliar with financial statement usage, this is a beginners trap. Don't get the columns mixed up! Record these figures in the form described above in the correct years in the correct column. Also make sure the number of digits you have recorded is the same for each year.

Capital K

Then move to the Balance Sheet in the Financial Statement.

What is Capital K? From the economic point of view, we are looking at the value of Capital used for productive purposes. A close proxy is Total Assets, as this is the value of the total capital used. (Net Assets which is Total Assets less Liabilities, or Equity, used by accountants, is not suitable as it is not a measure of the total productive capacity of the firm.)

The Total Assets figure is at the bottom of the Assets section of the Balance Sheet, and is the sum of the Current Assets and the Fixed Assets. Note the figures for two years, K_1 and K_2 in the above form. Make sure you get the figures from the correct years, and the digit numbers are the same.

As an aside, I have a misgiving about Total Assets being a totally suitable proxy for Capital, as accountants regularly revalue this figure, usually upwards, with the intention of massaging the published profits figure. In the case of Enron for example, this activity involved total duplicity. However I still continue to use the published figure for Total Assets for a reason – this Returns to Scale system has an inbuilt safety factor. If the Total Assets figure is excessively revised upwards, the α, the elasticity of revenue to capital, generally turns negative as it shows a less efficient use of capital. This is a warning not to invest in this company's shares.

Labor L

Scroll back up to the Revenue page, as the cost of Labor is conceptually deducted from Total Revenue to partly create the value of profits.

Finally Labor. This is a fraught subject. Under current accounting rules in most countries, companies are not compelled to publish wage costs or employee costs. Furthermore most companies, especially the larger one go to extreme efforts to hide their wage costs. You have to be a detective to find any useful figures on labor costs in any company accounts. Yet it is such an important figure. I feel strongly that the law should be changed compelling companies to publish their labor costs, the wages bill, in the costs section in the revenue statement.

What can you do? You have two options. Search the related published figures or use a suitable proxy.

Some companies, often I feel by mistake, publish their wages costs in the 'Notes' section. It is worth looking at the Index of the Notes, which is situated towards the end of the Financial Statement, and you may get referred to something called "Employee Benefits", or even if you are lucky "Employee Costs". Go to this area and see if there is a reference to Wage Costs, or something equivalent.

Otherwise you must use a Proxy. The labor expense figure you are looking for is buried in the 'costs' section of the Revenue Statement somewhere between Total Revenue and the estimated Profits. The best proxy that may appear in the Revenues section is 'Employee Benefits'. Most of this is wage costs, but there are other add-ons such as contributions to the pension fund, health insurance and so on. Nevertheless these can be called labor costs, and the on-costs normally closely match wages.

Most (but not all) Revenue pages can show some form of alternative to labor expenses. The ones I use are:

1 Employee Benefits
2 Administrative expenses
3 Sales expenses
4 Research expenses.
5 Selling, general and administrative expenses.
6 Costs of Goods Sold (COGS).

If Employee Benefits are not published, and the other items are, I normally add Administrative Expenses, Sales Expenses and Research Expenses together to use as a labor cost proxy. I have found that components of the above list provide a good proxy for total labor costs. My rationale is that the above three items provide a major proportion of the labor costs, and they rise at about the same rate as other hidden labor costs.

But I am aware I am missing a load of other labor expenses, often buried in Cost of Goods Sold. But as I said, companies won't publish wages cost unless compelled.

If the company also includes Cost of Goods Sold (COGS), add the figure to the above group. Wages are just one component of manufacturing expenses, there being raw materials and other expenses. But the proportion of wages in COGS is not likely to vary between the two years, so it is a suitable proxy to be added to wages costs.

Is this wage cost proxy process useful? Are the Returns to Scale figures you get at the end sufficiently accurate for you to base you investment decisions?

I have found that these expense figures are surprisingly accurate, for the reason that the hidden wage figure is usually a fixed ratio of these expense figures. Remember, you are not after numerical accuracy, but *proportions*. If the proportions of the expenses stay the same between years, the proportionate change of these expenses will be the same as the proportionate change in labor costs you are trying to use. In those cases where I have belatedly dug up the actual wages figure, the returns to scale results have changed, but not by an amount sufficient to change my investment decision on this company.

You can conduct a 'sensitivity analysis' to reassure yourself on this. Say you have managed to obtain two years' proxy labor costs, which you have put in a spreadsheet to obtain a certain returns to scale. Then reduce both proxy labor figures by a fixed proportion, say by half, and check to see if the result has a large effect on the returns to scale result. In most cases it will not make a significant difference.

A few companies publish an abbreviated revenue statement, which does not really explain how they reached their profits figure, and leave out any labor costs. The worst offenders are those who publish "Net Revenue" instead of "Total Revenue". Dig around to see if you can find an expanded expenses section. Otherwise if this is not forthcoming, my advice is to leave these companies well alone. There are a heap of companies you can invest in, honestly run, with dependable financial statements. You are not compelled to support the sleazes of this world.

CHAPTER SIX

ESTIMATING α AND β USING A SPREADSHEET

Which brings us to the next subject, estimating α and β.

Yes, I recommend using spreadsheets. Using a calculator is too tedious and error prone, while using some computer program is overdone, and also lacks the visible benefits of a spreadsheet layout.

An example of a spreadsheet is shown in the next chapter.

This spreadsheet in its simplest form consists of 10 columns.

The top row is the title row, naming each column. These are:

Column 1. Company Name
Column 2. Income Y1
Column 3. Capital K1
Column 4. Labor L1
Column 5. Income Y2
Column 6. Capital K2
Column 7. Labor L2
Column 8. Elasticity of revenue to capital α
Column 9. Elasticity of revenue to labor β
Column 10. Returns to Scale α + β

The spreadsheet can be expanded to make it easy for you, by having additional columns for the logs (ln) of each variable.

The formula for α in column 8 from above is

$$\alpha = \frac{\ln L_2 \ln Y_1 - \ln L_1 \ln Y_2}{\ln L_2 \ln K_1 - \ln L_1 \ln K_2}$$

If you are not skillful in inserting formulae in a spreadsheet, find some help. Most office workers nowadays are skilled in this. It is one of those basic office skills required nowadays!

The formula for β in column 9 from above is

$$\beta = \frac{\ln Y_1 - \alpha \ln K_1}{\ln L_1}$$

You get nearly the same result for substituting in the figures Y2, K2 and L2. Try it.

You have now got α and β. For column ten the returns to scale is

$$R = \alpha + \beta$$

How does one fill in the spreadsheet? So lets take our example of the table right at the start.

GENERAL ELECTRIC

	Y Income	K capital	L Labor
Year 1	147288	718189	54185
Year 2	147359	685328	53912

Under the title 'Company Name' in the first column insert the name 'General Electric'.

Under 'Income Y1' in the second column insert '147288'.

Under 'Capital K1' in the third column insert '718189'

Under 'Labor L1' in the fourth column insert '54185'

Under 'Income Y2' in the fifth column insert '147359'

Under Capital K2 in the sixth column insert '685328'

Under Labor L2 in the seventh column insert '53912'

You then insert the spreadsheet formulae in the next two columns.

A spreadsheet tip. As these formulae are complicated, it may be simpler for some to split the formulae up, and have separate columns for the logs of Y, A and L for both years, before doing the setting up the formula in a single column.

Then watch the magic unfold. Quickly the spreadsheet calculates the values for α, β, and α + β. You have got figures for the elasticity of revenue to capital, elasticity of revenue to labor, and returns to scale!

Just to check if you have this spreadsheet set out correctly, these are the figures that you should have obtained for α, β, and α + β.

α = -0.1

β = 1.3

α + β = 1.2

What does all this mean?

α + β is the measure of the returns to scale of General Electric, 1.2. Yes, it is operating under increasing returns to scale, but by not very much (I know many firms with a higher returns to scale). Constant returns to scale for comparison is 1.

But this measure is made up of two very disparate figures. α, the elasticity of revenue with respect to capital, is negative. This means that General Electric has inefficient use of capital. For every extra dollar invested in capital, total revenue <u>falls</u> 10 cents! Not a happy state of affairs.

β, the elasticity of revenue with respect to labor, is positive. This means that General Electric has efficient use of labor. For every extra dollar spent on wages, total revenue increases by $1 30 cents.

Effectively General Electric is being supported by its efficient labor force. Despite being a household name, under the criterion of returns to scale, General Electric is shown to be a not very good investment.

This is not an unusual situation among American firms, especially after the 2008 Financial Crisis. When interest rates were very low, large firms borrowed massive amounts at low interest, and those workers who keep their jobs are efficient.

In Europe, often the opposite takes place. The business capital is run very efficiently, but the workforce is inefficient. I often try to tell them to reduce their workforce!

Ideally for a well-run firm, both capital and labor should be efficient, and adding more than a dollar for every dollar invested. But many firms have an α and β each less than one though positive, and a returns to scale just over 1. Nearly constant returns to scale. They are just marking time!

What about the frequent demands to cut labor cost? Sometimes this is just the wrong thing to do. When β is greater than one, and accountants try to cut costs by cutting employees, this makes things worse! It reduces revenue disproportionately. But the bean counters never seem to realize it. Cutting staff only works when β is negative!

Similarly firms with negative α have to sell assets and reduce debt to improve their performance, something accountants rarely advise unless the firm is in desperate straits.

CHAPTER SEVEN

THE SPREADHEET RESULTS

The beauty and benefit of this Returns to Scale method is that with a spreadsheet you can get dozens of company results on one page. You can compare them against each other, sort the results into order of increasing returns to scale, and even manipulate the results by dividing them say by their current price/earnings ratios and re-sorting them.

This does away with the current investment selection method of going through tedious, and largely useless investment reports on each company. By the time you have read a dozen of these reports, you don't know how to make head or tail of them. Additionally there is no way to compare the companies, as each company will have at least half a dozen investment criteria, all different.

When you use the Returns to Scale methodology, all these criteria, at least all the relevant ones, are subsumed into one figure, the value of the Returns to Scale; with commentary on the efficiency of capital and labor derived from the estimated elasticities of revenue of capital and labor, α and β.

On the next page is an example of a Returns to Scale spreadsheet. Yes, they are genuine company results. But a word of warning. By the time you read this book all these figures will be out of date, as they largely relate to the first half of the year 2013. Do not use these figures for your investment decisions. They are published for instructional purposes only. You must produce your own spreadsheet based on the latest Annual Reports, and of course, keep them up to date. However, a week's solid work should give at least 300 or 400 results to choose from.

I suggest that you use as a guide for a list of quoted companies a publication such as the Fortune 500 list, and obtain from elsewhere your own financial information for each company. (The Fortune 500 list unfortunately has limited financial information).

You will however have to set up your own spreadsheet. Unfortunately I can't stick an electronic gizmo into this book to do it for you. But I intend to set up a web site, with a spreadsheet, which you can copy. Just do a Google search and it should pop up. And yes, it will be free. And no, this is not intended to be a moneymaking scheme.

Get the working of your spreadsheet checked by someone who knows these things. You don't want to make the wrong investment decisions because you set up the formulae wrong.

Table 1

SPREADSHEET EXAMPLE
RETURNS TO SCALE CALCULATIONS FOR A GROUP OF SELECTED COMPANIES
IF YOU GET THE SAME α AND β IN YOUR SPREADSHEET USING THESE INPUTS, IT WORKS!

Company name	Y1 Income Year1	K1 Capital Year 1	L1 Wages Year 1	Y2 Income Year 2	K2 Capital Year 2	L2 Wages Year 2	α	β	α+β Returns to Scale
American Express	33776	153140	6597	34932	153375	6171	1.22402419	-0.4760149	0.74800932
Apple	65225	75183	7299	108249	116371	10028	3.08167977	-2.6434194	0.4382604
BP	375765	146323	12327	379136	151457	13117	1.72300583	-0.8127752	0.91023064
Caterpillar	2693	34742	416	2783	35138	427	0.03856612	1.24283971	1.28414053
Chevron	253706	209474	26394	241909	232982	27294	-1.3422061	2.83758212	1.49537601
Coca cola	46542	79974	28327	48017	86174	28964	0.15713499	0.87539188	1.02953312
Disney	36149	63117	30452	38063	69206	31337	0.36579396	0.62499372	0.99078768
Du Pont	36144	51499	29142	35310	49859	32252	0.91023828	0.0602924	0.97053068
General Electric	147288	718189	54185	147359	685328	53912	-0.1477419	1.27451065	1.12676873
General Motors	150276	144603	130386	152256	149422	140236	1.48987957	-0.4909167	0.99896271
IBM	127245	116433	55533	104507	119213	53122	0.9597094	0.0352159	0.99492475
Intel	53999	71119	36262	53441	84351	28395	0.56064949	0.44130797	1.00195747
JP Morgan Chase	97031	2359141	30585	96606	2415689	30810	0.72075302	0.08563921	0.80639223
Microsoft	73723	121271	38237	77849	142431	30836	0.70990355	0.27459901	0.98450256
Pepsi	66504	72882	31593	65492	74638	31291	-0.1473905	1.23112345	1.08373294
Shell	470171	345257	14335	467153	360325	14616	-1.9543108	3.96870283	2.01439207

WARNING. These figures are out of date by the time you get them. DO NOT use these figures to make investment decisions.

Many will be shocked by these results. Their favorite shares, recommended by their stockbrokers, get the thumbs down, or at the very best, are a mediocre investment.

Well don't complain to me! As I said, these results are out of date. Re-estimate them yourself, using the latest Annual Report results.

However, one thing about these published numbers is that they are calculated correctly. If you plug these numbers into your own spreadsheet, you should get identical answers. This demonstrates that your spreadsheet works! Then you can modify these numbers with the latest figures.

This is the basic spreadsheet. For beginning users of spreadsheets I suggest that you spread it out by having separate columns for the logs of Y1, K1, L1, Y2, K2, L2. This should simplify the final formulae.

Note – the logs you must use in your spreadsheet are the <u>exponential</u> logs, 'ln'; NOT the logs to the base 10, 'log'.

CHAPTER EIGHT

BUYING SHARES, MAINTAINING AND UPDATING YOUR PORTFOLIO

So you have done your research (yeech!), constructed a massive spreadsheet, and from this you have selected a list of suitable shares you are interested in investing in. Well done!

Yes, you can go out in a fit of enthusiasm and buy a selection of these chosen shares. There is no harm in doing that, though check the p/e ratios. But lets assume that you have a heap of cash and want to construct an 'optimal portfolio'. Just to get the last ounce of investment gain out of the system. How do you do that?

Basically you need to buy shares in proportion to their measures of returns to scale, and in inverse proportion to their relative price. The higher the returns to scale, the more shares you buy, and higher the relative price the fewer shares you buy. (I won't go into such issues as the variability of the share prices, beta, and so on. This is for a 'do it yourself' portfolio, and the suggested method is in my opinion perfectly adequate for most investment portfolios under $100 million.)

What is the best measure of relative price? Obviously there is a vast range of share prices, depending on the units of their shares.

There are many measures that are independent of the unit of the shares such as the price earnings ratio (p/e), or the dividend yield, or earnings to cash ratio, and so on. I have found by far the best measure of price is the p/e ratio, and the foregoing discussion will be conducted in terms of the p/e ratio. But don't let this stop you using another measure according to your needs. Just substitute this measure into the term p/e ratio in the foregoing discussion. The methodology will work just the same.

So. More work. (sigh!). Another spreadsheet. (groan!).

This spreadsheet will be much smaller and simpler than the previous one. But three major advantages will stem from its use.

1. The distribution of shares in your portfolio will have a distribution biased towards shares that are the most likely to increase in price.
2. It incorporates a system of regularly revising and renewing the share portfolio.
3. And lastly, described in a later chapter, it incorporates a 'trip wire', which tells you when to liquidate the share portfolio into cash at the height of a share boom, before it crashes. These share crashes are regular occurrences, yet people rely on nothing more than instinct for choosing the time when to bail out. As a consequence most lose out!

Right. Lets set up this spreadsheet. It consists of eight columns. 1. Company name. 2. The latest returns to scale measure of the company. 3. The latest p/e ratio of company (obtained from an alternative source such as a newspaper). 4. The ratio of the returns to scale divided of the company by the p/e ratio of the company. 5. Percentage weight of each share. 6. Actual value of these shares.. 7. Desired weighted value of each share. 8. Difference. Sell –. Buy +.

This spreadsheet is shown in the diagram below.

Company name	Returns to scale of company	Latest p/e ratio of company	Returns to scale of the company/pe ratio of the company	Percentage desired weight of the holding of each share %	Actual value of all the shares held of this company $	Desired weighted value of all the shares held of this company $	Difference. Sell –. Buy +.

The explanation of these column names is as follows:

Company name	Name of the company shares
Returns to scale of company	The calculated returns to scale of that company*
P/e ratio of company	Current p/e ratio of that company obtained from a daily media source
Returns to scale of company/pe ratio of company	The ratio of the returns to scale divided by the pe ratio
Percentage desired weight of the holding of each share	This percentage weight ratio is obtained by dividing the above

	obtained ratio by the sum of all the ratios in the portfolio, and converting it into a percentage figure
Actual value of each of all the shares held of this company	Number of that company's shares in the portfolio x current market price
Desired weighted value of all the shares held of this company	The desired weighted value of each share is obtained by multiplying the percentage weight of each share by the current portfolio value of all the shares in the portfolio (sum of actual value of each of these shares in the portfolio)
Difference. Sell –. Buy +.	This is the value of the shares of that company which should be sold or bought to restore the portfolio to an 'optimum' distribution. It is found by subtracting the actual value of each of these shares from the desired weighted value of each of these shares.

* To save a bit of effort, a link for the returns to scale measure can be connected to the previous spreadsheet. So when that figure changes, so does the one in this spreadsheet change.

So there you are. This spreadsheet may look complicated, but if you can't set it up yourself, ask a person moderately competent in spreadsheets to construct it.

But as I said constructing and maintaining this spreadsheet is well worth the effort. You will be immediately on top of all your share investments. Furthermore you will automatically buy and sell shares when necessary.

When you initially purchase your portfolio of shares, I recommend that you use this spreadsheet to allocate the proportions of each share you will purchase for the portfolio. As you see, by dividing by the p/e ratio, there is a bias towards the less expensive shares. There is a very good reason for this. Less expensive shares, with lower p/e ratios, are more likely to rise in price! So are shares with higher returns to scale. Thus your portfolio is biased towards shares of companies with higher returns to scale and lower p/e ratios.

Now, how often should your portfolio be revised?

This should be done regularly, at least every six months for a small portfolio, and more frequently for a large portfolio.

However the Returns to Scale for each company should be recalculated as soon as its Annual Report is published. This is important as it happens quite often that a large change in the returns to scale measure has occurred. Usually for the worst. What happens is that after a good year, management often gets a rush of blood to the head, and starts splashing out on assets, or hiring staff like mad. If this happens it is best to reduce your holding of these shares immediately before the rest of the world realizes. You will probably be selling shares that have significantly appreciated, as of course in this Annual Report the company has announced significantly improved performance. So re-weight the holding using the method described above, and reduce your holding. If you are in a hurry, just reduce the share by the ratio of the old and new returns to scale measure, and do a general re-weighting later.

During the writing of this book, an event occurred which demonstrated how important it is to re-estimate the returns to scale of each company as soon as you receive the annual financial report. About a year ago, part of my recommended portfolio was the shares a firm called the Forge Group, a company mainly involved in servicing machinery for mining companies, but it also did some construction work. It operated around the world. I had placed it in various portfolios as its returns to scale at the time was around 2, and it appeared to be a very efficiently run and prosperous company. Anyway the re-calculations from the figures derived from the last annual report saw the returns to scale drop to below one. Declining returns to scale. I automatically eliminated Forge Group from the investment portfolios.

Nearly a year later the company went bankrupt. The downturn in the mining sector, plus the previous effects of over-expansion detected by the returns to scale calculations, had done Forge in. The moral of this tale is that the process of immediate re-calculation of returns to scale after the

Annual Report has been released must not be neglected. These calculations invariably detect changes in the operations in the company, and if used with the portfolio method described above, will probably get you out in time if things go bad. I sold at around $4. The share price dropped to zero within nine months.

The aim of regularly reweighting the portfolio is to automatically readjust the portfolio for both changes in price and changes in returns to scale. In most cases minor changes can maintain an optimal mix of the existing shares in the portfolio.

I also recommend a system of constant renewal of the share portfolio. I have found this is a very necessary exercise. It is too easy to rest on one's laurels. Out with the old and in with the new!

I remove the shares with the lowest returns to scale/pe ratios, and replace them with shares with better ratios. Up to five shares every six months in a thirty share portfolio.

I usually do this on a regular, not continuous, basis as you have to adjust the proportions of all the shares in the portfolio at the same time. There is a big question of stockbrokers' commissions. For portfolios up to a million dollars once every six months is enough.

If I find a 'good' investment with a high ratio, I usually don't buy immediately, but I add it to a list to be used on the regular revision date. But this is up to you.

A question may be asked, are price earnings ratios the best divisors? You are welcome to use others. But I have found over time that price earnings ratios are one of the best measures of share relative value (though not of course a measure of whether the share is worth buying. Returns to scale is far superior).

CHAPTER NINE

DO SHARE PRICES ALWAYS INCREASE FOR HIGH RETURNS TO SCALE COMPANIES?

This is the elephant in the room. Do share prices always rise when those companies have a high returns to scale?

In the vast majority of cases, yes. But not always. For the following reasons:

1. The market overall may be a bear market, and all share prices are going down. Under those circumstances even share prices of shares in high returns to scale companies will go down. As described in Chapter 10, if you follow the advice given in that Chapter, you will already have sold out. If you are just starting, my advice is wait and start buying when the market has hit the bottom.
2. The market is not rational, it is often ignorant, and can sometimes (though not very often) overlook the shares of a highly profitable company with increasing profits. Especially if the company is relatively small.
3. There may be a short or long term prejudice against that company. It may churn out profits and dividends to kingdom come, and investors won't touch those shares. Tobacco companies. Manufacturers of firearms (I won't touch them). Manufacturers of condoms and sex aids. Alcohol. Exploited labor. For a long time I refused to invest in South African mining companies, and I sold out again recently when one mine used guns on its striking workers. You name it. Always check what the firm does, and if you have a moral concern don't invest. You won't be alone.
4. The company operates in a very risky area, such as mining companies in Bolivia, and investors rightly avoid them.
5. The p/e is already high, and the shares have already had a recent 'run up'. This is not a reason for refusing to buy the shares. If the returns to scale/p e ratio is high enough, there could be still a place in the portfolio for this share, to that proportion calculated as described above.
6. The share market has crashed, gone into a complete funk for a while, war has broken out, your country has been invaded, hit by a

devastating earthquake/tsunami. All these are classified by insurers 'acts of god'. Wait, and later pick up the pieces. One thing is guaranteed. Your portfolio of shares is better than most others' and is likely to recover faster.

My overall experience is that, using this returns to scale method, you will tend to invest in small and mediums sized firms, not large ones. The firms you select with high returns to scale are profitable and growing fast. When you buy the shares, hopefully the shares will tend to be relatively cheap. As the firms grow, they will tend to come more onto the general investment horizon and share prices will rise.

Is investing in shares in small and medium sized companies riskier than investing solely in large company shares and 'blue chips'? The answer is no, if you have a share portfolio, and the number of shares in your portfolio exceeds 30 or more.

Why? Back to economics. The increased number of shares in your portfolio reduces the overall risk of your portfolio. For a portfolio of 30 or more risky shares, the risk is reduced, and is in fact nearly as safe as a portfolio of 30 or more 'safe' or 'blue chip' shares. This counterintuitive conclusion was first discovered by the economist Harry Markowitz in the 1950's, used by Michael Millken to create his 'junk bond' empire in the 1980's, and misused more recently to bundle risky mortgages into 'CDOs'. But for a portfolio of shares the level of 'systemic' risk is not much difference between a portfolio of medium sized company shares and a same sized portfolio of 'blue chips'. But don't go to extremes, buying shares of risky mining companies in the Congo, as you think a portfolio of this type of shares is safe. Use your common sense.

I suppose this is a good place for a **Disclaimer**. If the method I have described in this book is applied conscientiously and the methodology is completely followed without error; over the medium term with an adequate portfolio of shares, losses are likely to be minimized and profits are likely to be made. The author does not guarantee that you will not make losses in all circumstances, or will make profits at a particular period. Markets are not completely rational over short periods of time, and 'acts of god' and extreme events beyond the control of any person can occur. You are solely responsible for all the investment decisions you make. This book only describe a general method to make good investments, and provides no advice on individual shares beyond indicating a way to select good share investments and allocating the selected share into a proportion of your share portfolio.

CHAPTER TEN

AVOIDING RUIN, OR AT LEAST THE HARMFUL EFFECTS OF A GENERAL SHARE CRASH

What! Avoid ruin! I thought this method you describe almost guarantees that you will make money. What is this talk about ruin?

Yes, dear reader, that is correct. But you will have noticed that on average every ten years the share market goes into a frenzy, rises to a peak (very nice), and then suddenly without warning crashes 30 or 40% (not so nice). All those shares you bought at or near the peak have lost money. How devastating!

A rational reader would say to me, well that is not your fault. After all, the aim of the book is to teach you to pick good shares, with the not inconsiderable hope that they will rise in price. The periodic share crashes are beyond anyone's control.

True, that is one way of looking at it. However, dear reader, I DO want to see you retire to a prosperous old age, and if you have got this far, and have applied the methodology which I have described, I will feel guilty if I have left you with a situation where periodically all your hard work comes to (near) naught, and you have to wait several years for recovery. That is the usual fate of all share investors, even if they have invested well.

But don't be dismayed. I shall finish this chapter with a description of an automatic signal, a trip wire, which will save your hard earned earnings before a market crash. Read carefully.

First of all, you have noticed that you have a method of automatically selling shares from your portfolio shares with a high relative p/e value, and re-basing your portfolio.

But what happens when all the shares in the portfolio have a high p/e value? No matter how hard you try, everything in your portfolio seems to be traded up to the sky? Then it is the time to get out. Cash up. Put the money into government bonds (if the return is 4% p.a. or more). Sit on it. Wait.

What level should you sell? I have a magic figure. If the average p/e of your portfolio is **20** or more, sell the lot. This will give a buffer for risk.

Why twenty?

When a p/e is 20, the earnings rate of return to capitalization is 5%. This is equal to the 'risk free' rate of return of long-term government stocks. Even with a potential further rise in portfolio values it is not worth taking this risk. Remember you are playing with your retirement money.

Surely most shares in your portfolio at the top of the bubble will have a p/e greater than 20? Not just half, most.

Here, bear with me, as I go into a bit more economic speak, or you can jump ahead and just do what I say. The average p/e is matter of the distribution of p/e's in your portfolio, and the shape of that distribution. Remember you have been selling a high proportion of the shares with a relatively high p/e and buying shares with a low p/e.

Imagine a chart of the p/e's of the shares in your portfolio as a graph with the measure of the p/e's as the x axis, and the value of shares as the y axis. The graph will be in the form of a curve, with the highest point to the left, and descending to the right. The shares with the lowest p/e's will have the most invested in them. Why? Because you have been regularly re-basing your portfolio, so that most of the money in the portfolio is in shares with a low p/e.

Thus the average p/e will not be in the middle of the curve, the average p/e of all the shares, but moved to the left, the weighted value of the p/e's.

What do you mean by "average"? I mean the "weighted average", weighted by the total value of each share in your portfolio. How do you weight the shares?
1. Multiply the value of each share by the p/e of that share.
2. Add all these products together.
3. Add up the actual values of all the shares in the portfolio to obtain a total.
4. Now this is important, divided the weighted total above by the second portfolio total to get a weighted average p/e.

It's not hard. You can actually set up the spreadsheet to do it for you each time.

So, when the weighted average p/e of your continuously revised returns to scale portfolio, constructed in the method described above, reaches 20, SELL ALL.

The majority of the share in your portfolio will have a p/e of over 20, and will be over priced.

From long experience, the mean long term p/e of shares are something like 15. This is your warning bell. Soon, very soon, the share market will crash. DON'T get greedy and hang on!

Alternatively just add up all the p/e's in your portfolio and divide by the number of shares in the portfolio. As described above you will get an upward bias in the average p/e, but that is an error on the safe side. Sell if the average p/e of the portfolio is above 20.

CHAPTER ELEVEN

ON THE QUESTION OF FINDING SHARES TO INVEST IN, SHARE TIPS, DIVIDENDS, AND ASSORTED FURTHER ADVICE

How does one find new shares to invest in?

You have started by using the massive spreadsheet method at the start. It is the sledgehammer approach, but after you have analyzed the Top 500 you have picked up a few shares to invest in. No, you don't want to go through that process again, unless you are that unusual person that loves doing that sort of thing. But you have gained two major assets:

1. Knowledge that the vast majority of the top 500 companies are investment junk, and are not worth investing in.
2. You have a spreadsheet that will work out the returns to scale of any new company you will find.

However, if you want to keep going for another 10,000 quoted companies, don't let me stop you. This chapter is aimed at other readers who want to stay sane.

So you have done the Top 500. But there are loads of others. How do you hear about them?

Free tips? No! If you get a free tip from some public source as an internet site, newspaper article, or TV or radio program, you are either at the end of the line or somebody else wants to sell and wants the bunnies to support the market. Very very occasionally the tipsters pass out something good, but only to maintain their record "I recommended so-and-so which increased 40%!" All these tips are worth checking with this returns to scale methodology, but don't hold your breath.

Investment magazines, and paid for investment advice services, whether internet or hard copy, especially specialist ones, are a better bet. It is worthwhile subscribing. On the subject of subscriptions I know many investors who are personally "cheap". They won't spend money on subscriptions, either paper or the internet. Now paid for investment tips are vastly more valuable than the free variety, for the simple reason that the writers of these have to perform to make a living. It is better to subscribe to a service for a limited period, and test the recommendations, than not subscribe at all. If at the end of 12 months, if the service does not come up to desired quality, give them a chop. As a rule of thumb, I have unsubscribed about half of the internet investment services I have signed up for. And about ten per cent of the hard copy magazines.

As for the 'cheap' investors who won't subscribe to investment services, they lose most of their money in the end. If you go near them, they complain, and blame anyone but himself or herself.

Other sources of investment ideas are serendipity. A news report mentions a company in a particular context. Write it down. A friend mentions a share. It is amazing how many good investment ideas pop up this way. But always check them out using the spreadsheet.

Finally your stockbroker. Well the dear old stockbroker has a job to do. Buy, buy, buy. The firm lives on commissions. There is always a "story". Every week in fact. Test all their recommendations. You will find most are junk. A minority are bad junk, the sort which tempts you to ring up and abuse your broker. Don't. The poor guy is only doing his job. Occasionally, very occasionally, your stockbroker comes up with something good. Keep them happy with a bit of commission. But for re-balancing, I recommend using a low commission broker. High commissions can eat into your fund.

I also subscribe to a service that notifies me if a share price in the vast galaxy of shares out there has jumped a bit. No you don't need a "reason" for the jump. Somebody knows something. It is worth checking it out. If stripped of "advice" it is a cheap service, and well worth it. It is amazing how many good and interesting shares swim into view using this service.

You will notice that throughout this book, I have not mentioned dividends and yields. There is a simple reason for this. The purpose of this investment strategy is to invest for capital gains. Don't invest for dividends unless you really need the income. There are a number of reasons for this.
1. Capital gains obtained using this method are several times the maximum expected dividend of even the most profitable company. It is rare for a yield to exceed 6 or 7 per cent, while expected capital gains for individual shares using this method can exceed 25

per cent per annum. From simple arithmetic, if you had a choice of investing for dividends or capital gains, which should you do?
2. Dividends, if they end up in your bank account, usually get spent. (How many investors' spouses grab the money and spend it before you think about what you are going to do with it!). Capital gains usually get reinvested and compounded into that all important retirement fund,
3. Often a 'ten bagger' as they call it, also issues dividends, or increases them, though that is not the original investment intention. You win both sides.

Conclusion

The purpose of this book was to improve your economic welfare. But not in some zero-sum way, through short-term speculation. You need to select shares of companies that will increase in value in the medium term. The way to select these companies is to select those that operate under increasing returns to scale. Their profits will increase over time, and given a rational share market, the share prices of these companies will increase over time.

If all companies resolved to operate under increasing returns to scale at all times, the welfare of the entire economy and society would be improved. Waste would be reduced, economic growth would increase, and as a result unemployment would fall and wages rise. All the result of the application of a little formula!

But I don't suppose you have a major concern about the general economic welfare. All you are basically concerned about is how much money you are going to make.

Now a good fund manager makes in the long term a growth in the value of the share portfolio he/she manages of around 5% per annum over the inflation rate. That is a good one. Bad ones do far worse, and indeed lose vast sums of their investors' money.

Most funds, if you look at the MorningStar reports, are run by bad or mediocre investment managers. Their returns are consistently bad, far worse than the return provided by the apocryphal monkey throwing darts at a list of shares. Some even, those funds run by banks, deliberately make a bad return by investing their clients money in their banks' deposits. So in many cases you cannot even depend on the best intentions or honesty of your fund managers. They are all overpaid, and the vast majority do not give a good return for our money.

It is far better that you did the investing yourself, if you could be nearly certain that the method you use produces better than normal returns. Then all you need worry about is the commission costs of regularly re-balancing your portfolio. (A job that you must do).

So what are the returns from this "Increasing Returns to Scale " method? I am tempted to make a claim for the 'average' portfolio gain. But that can be dangerous because everyone's portfolio, personal competence, and application will be different. What I will say is that the vast majority of high returns to scale company shares found with a p/e ratio of around 14 (yes they appear all the time) in a short time increase to a p/e of 18 to 20. That is an increase in value of 25%. Over the longer term the gains are greater.

Now, I don't want to get letters from investors who used this method who tell me "Last year, after the market dropped 25 per cent, my portfolio only broke even!. I should have used that charting method advised by my brother in law."

Yes, there are charting methods that do work. Without a doubt. Most don't, but a few do. But there is a downside to using the charting method. It will take up a lot of your time. All of your spare time, in fact. The charting method only works if you spend every evening at your screen checking the current charts for you entire portfolio. Your eyes will go red! Automatically generated signals? You have to re-set them every couple of days. Employing someone else to check the charts? Even the most conscientious employees have 'personal problems' from time to time, which just happen to coincide with the phases of the moon and a big loss for you. Don't I know it! No, from my bitter experience, charting is a route to madness.

No. Medium to long term investing is the only way to go. And if you are going to go down that route, you can either do a Warren Buffet, and churn through a really massive amount of accounting information to get to a single nugget, or do it the "Returns to Scale" method. Churn through much less accounting information, just three sets of data per company, and that way you have a much higher probability of striking a lot of nuggets. You will have a plethora of choice from which you can choose a high performance portfolio.

Tax. Yes, like death, it is unavoidable. Trying to evade tax is not only illegal, and tax evaders are pursued relentlessly by every government in the world, but the process of evading tax destroys your peace of mind and happiness, as you have constantly in the back of your mind, correctly, that you are being pursued and may be caught and severely punished. It's not worth it. Tax avoidance, the legal sort, is also not worth it. Going through the contortions and expense is equally soul destroying. Living abroad and away from your natural home to avoid tax is silly. Realize that you gain from the protection and welfare of your government and be happy to pay any tax charge fully to pay for that privilege. You are making a lot of money. Paying full taxes on your profits won't send you broke in most tax regimes.

CHAPTER TWELVE

EXCURSIS, OR HOW COMPANIES CAN ACHIEVE INCREASING RETURNS TO SCALE, AND VALETE

I considered dropping this chapter, as it provides no information on investing. It is really an economist's discussion of issues raised by this returns to scale method. If you wish to give this chapter a miss, please do so. You won't miss anything relevant to investing. Otherwise gratify this excursion of an economist.

Getting your firm to operate on increasing returns to scale

So the CEO of your company tells you to find out how your company can achieve increasing returns to scale. He has discovered that the market values the shares of companies with increasing returns to scale more highly, and his remuneration includes shares and options in the company.

How do you do it?

Lets start with General Electric. The previous figures are…

	Y Income	K capital	L Labor
Year 1	147288	718189	54185
Year 2	147359	685328	53912

The CEO wishes to achieve a returns to scale of at least 1.5. Your aim is to calculate estimate the required level of capital, labor and income to achieve this.

You can try reworking the formula, plugging in the returns to scale and a new set of values. I can tell you now that you will obtain some very extreme results! This is for a reason I will go in to.

Alternatively you can try playing around with the figures in the spreadsheet for the second year of General Electric, and do a simulation. One possible result is shown below.

	Y Income	K capital	L Labor
Year 1	147288	718189	54185
Year 2	180000	660000	55000

This gives a returns to scale measure of 1.5.

Now when you are doing this simulation, it will become apparent that there are wild swings in the results, most of which cause a reduced returns to scale. If you keep doing this simulation it should become apparent to you that there is only a very narrow path towards increasing returns to scale.

This is not the fault of the model. This process shows that firms operate on what economists call a 'knife edge'. There is only a very narrow path to success, and for smaller firms, for survival. Why do firms stay on this path? In brief, because they have learned to. Their internal culture rapidly learns what they should and should not do. Larger firms operate in what is called 'homeostasis'. Before they learn this, smaller firms can and do very rapidly fall off the cliff! (Steve Jobs ascribed the survival of his company to the fact that he accumulated cash reserves equal to the annual salaries of all the employees.)

The moral of this story for investors is – check the Annual Reports as soon as they come out!

Are smaller firms are more likely to operate under increasing returns to scale?

Most gains from returns to scale occur with smaller companies, but it is only with iron discipline that the stay on this track. A good example was Apple. It was achieving returns to scale up between 1.5 and 2 for several years running. However its latest result gave it a returns to scale of 0.4, with $\alpha = 3.08$, and $\beta = -2.64$. While Apple's financial management remained excellent despite complaints that it had retained too much cash, it got soft on the personnel side and hired too many people. But the returns to scale calculations gave excellent advance warning of a downturn in profits and performance of the company, and gave a very good signal to get out while the price was high and before the rush to sell.

I suggest for a firm the size of General Electric, if it wishes to achieve increasing returns to scale, that it split itself into a number of smaller divisions, each the size of a small company.

Why is a small firm more likely to operate under increasing returns to sale than a large one? The answer is that a small firm has more efficient and faster information flows inside the firm. It is likely to be more responsive to events and influences that can divert it from the path of increasing returns to scale. Some of theses influences can be internal – management is always trying to increase capital expenditure or the number employed, as they see, correctly, that there is a direct relation between increasing these variables and increased revenue and profits. But in the dire words of Edgar Allen Poe, this increase is "not enough".

Is there a maximum size for increasing returns to scale?

In empirical terms, what is the maximum size of a firm that can operate under increasing returns to scale? It varies. It can vary from five branches of certain banks I have investigated to one of the largest corporations in the world, in the case of Apple. As far as I can see, this variation does not depend on the nature of the industry the firm operates in, or manufacturing requirements (the traditional "scale" measure), but how the firm is organized. Communication has to be fast and accurate in the upward direction, and actions have to be fast, correct, and effective in the downward direction. For large firms, a strong and capable leader helps, whether it is Steve Jobs or Jack Welch. I noticed that Apple immediately went to pieces as soon as Steve Jobs died. Whatever he did could not be replicated. Maybe when the "science" of management develops, it can be developed on a framework that answers the question, "How do you keep a large company operating on increasing returns to scale?"

However large firms can and do operate under operate under increasing returns to scale. Royal Dutch Shell, for example, had a returns to scale of 2.01, with $\alpha = -1.95$ and $\beta = 3.96$. Its financial statistics were

ROYAL DUTCH SHELL

	Y Income	K capital	L Labor
Year 1	470171	345257	14335
Year 2	467153	360325	14616

Shell makes far more effective use of labor, though its use of capital is also much better in proportion to income than General Electric's. Gaining returns to scale is essentially dependent on the efficient use both capital and labor. One explanation is that Shell's management is excellent. It recruits graduates from Oxford and Cambridge with First Class Degrees, and then seeds them in at senior management levels, on the lines of the old colonial Indian Civil Service. I am very impressed with Shell senior managers. They are far better than the ones who "work their way up" in American firms, even those with MBA's.

Over the course of time I hope a behavioral change will occur in companies. They will start aiming to operate under increasing returns to scale.

On the question of profits – the most commonly used measure of success

The requirement to operate under increasing returns to scale will cause a major and painful change in management attitude. It is all too easy to achieve increased sales (and a declining rate of profitability) by increasing scale – by increasing assets and the labor force. But that is not good, even in the medium term, for the company as a whole. "Profit maximization" assumes constant returns to scale, teetering on the edge of falling profits as scale is increased. The glib economists' mantra "all firms must profit maximize" necessarily assumes the outcome of a fixed and stable economy, with all firms operating on constant returns to scale.

In actual fact all firms, dear reader, must maximize the *expected present value* of current and future profits - something quite different. They often sacrifice current profits for increased future profits. They don't maximize current profits.

My own mantra is, "all firms must constantly increase profits by remaining in the parameters of increasing returns to scale".

As for economic theory, many economists say that operating on increasing returns to scale is wrong, as all firms do or should "profit maximize". I won't disappear down that theoretical rabbit hole, except to point out that the concept of "profit maximization" beloved by all economists is grossly simplified, and indeed theoretically wrong. This is because the theoretical proof requiring profit maximization to be welfare maximizing implicitly requires constant returns to scale. (Look it up).

Firms in reality do not attempt to maximize current profits. What all firms do is attempt to maximize *"the present value of expected future profits",* which is not the same as maximizing current profits. They can and do trade lower current profits for higher expected future profits (which economists don't like, as it is not "profit maximization") to maximize the present value of expected future profits. They can do this by operating on increasing returns to scale. As I said, theoretically current profit maximization requires constant returns to scale.

The Kenneth Arrow concept of market optimization falls apart if constant returns to scale is not assumed. One of my pet complaints in economic theory is that the concept of constant returns to scale implicitly or explicitly pervades the entire theoretical structure. Economic theory needs to be thoroughly re-written to include the concept of increasing returns to scale (some elements of decreasing returns to scale are already included). But I am sure you have had too much economics already.

Farewell

So Valete! Remember there is no substitute for hard work, and a conscientious approach to share investing. Re-read the above chapters, and conscientiously apply the instructions. No short cuts, No, "I know better." When you get rich you can employ at least two others to do the hard work (so that they check each other). But even so, what you get out is what you put in. You, and only you.

I don't need to wish you best of luck, as that is not involved in this method. But I wish you prosperity and a prosperous old age.

CHAPTER 13

A MORE COMPLETE MATHEMATICAL EXPLANATION

Back to first principles.

The Cobb Douglas production function for increasing returns to scale is:

$Y = DK^{\alpha}L^{\beta}$

Where $D = Ac^{\alpha}c^{\beta}$

Now for two successive periods

$Y_1 = D_1 K_1^{\alpha_1} L_1^{\beta_1}$

$Y_2 = D_2 K_2^{\alpha_2} L_2^{\beta_2}$

Turning the above formulae into logarithmic form

$\text{Ln } Y_1 = \alpha_1 \ln K_1 + \beta_1 \ln L_1 + \ln D_1$

$\text{Ln } Y_2 = \alpha_2 \ln K_2 + \beta_2 \ln L_2 + \ln D_2$

If you assume that there is not much change in the value of D between the two years, as the operational structure of the firm does not change much between the two years, then $\ln D_1 - \ln D_2 = 0$.

So

$\text{Ln } Y_1 = \alpha_1 \ln K_1 + \beta_1 \ln L_1$

$\text{Ln } Y_2 = \alpha_2 \ln K_2 + \beta_2 \ln L_2$

Then

$\beta_1 \ln L_1 = \ln Y_1 - \alpha_1 \ln K_1$

$$\beta_2 \ln L_1 = \ln Y_2 - \alpha_2 \ln K_2$$

So

$$\beta_1 = \frac{\ln Y_1 - \alpha_1 \ln K_1}{\ln L_1}$$

$$\beta_2 = \frac{\ln Y_2 - \alpha_2 \ln K_2}{\ln L_2}$$

Now we assume $\beta_1 = \beta_2$ and $\alpha_1 = \alpha_2$, as we assume that there is little change in company structure between two years.

Thus

$$\beta = \frac{\ln Y_1 - \alpha \ln K_1}{\ln L_1}$$
$$\beta = \frac{\ln Y_2 - \alpha \ln K_2}{\ln L_2}$$

(In actual practice, the estimated values of β_1 and β_2 are usually very similar)

Then $\quad \dfrac{\ln Y_1 - \alpha \ln K_1}{\ln L_1} = \dfrac{\ln Y_2 - \alpha \ln K_2}{\ln L_2}$

$$(\ln Y_1 - \alpha \ln K_1)\ln L_2 = (\ln Y_2 - \alpha \ln K_2)\ln L_1$$

$$\ln Y_1 \ln L_2 - \alpha \ln K_1 \ln L_2 = \ln Y_2 \ln L_1 - \alpha \ln K_2 \ln L_1$$

$$\alpha \ln K_2 \ln L_1 - \alpha \ln K_1 \ln L_2 = \ln Y_2 \ln L_1 - \ln Y_1 \ln L_2$$

$$\alpha (\ln K_2 \ln L_1 - \ln K_1 \ln L_2) = \ln Y_2 \ln L_1 - \ln Y_1 \ln L_2$$

$$\alpha = \frac{\ln Y_2 \ln L_1 - \ln Y_1 \ln L_2}{\ln K_2 \ln L_1 - \ln K_1 \ln L_2}$$

Now, we have made some what is called heroic assumptions. That is $\alpha_1 = \alpha_2$, $\beta_1 = \beta_2$, and $\ln D_1 - \ln D_2 = 0$. Would this assumption be born out by an empirical experiment?

The experiment would be a multiple regression using the function

$$\text{Ln } Y = \alpha \ln K + \beta \ln L + \ln \delta$$

The aim of the regression would be to estimate the values of α and β, and the value of $\ln \delta$, the intercept in this regression, which is the value of $\ln D$.

The aim of the exercise would be to see if α and β differ significantly over two successive years, and that ($\ln \delta_1 - \ln \delta_2$) is not significantly different from zero.

If this checks out, the methodology is correct, and can be used to estimate the values of returns to scale for each company. NOTE. This methodology does NOT necessarily assume D=1. It may equal 1, but the individual D's, the measure of total factor productivity of the firm, are unlikely to.

Two separate regressions were run of the form

$$\text{Ln } Y_1 = \ln \delta_1 + \alpha \ln K_1 + \beta \ln L_1$$

$$\text{Ln } Y_2 = \ln \delta_2 + \alpha \ln K_2 + \beta \ln L_2$$

for the same data set with two successive years.

The data set variables were called r1, k1, l1 and r2, k2, l2 for the two successive years where $r = \ln Y$, $k = \ln K$, $l = \ln L$, with subscripts for the respective years.

The regression formulae were

$$r_1 = \text{intersect}_1 + \alpha_1 k_1 + \beta_1 l_1$$

and

$$r_2 = \text{intersect}_2 + \alpha_2 k_1 + \beta_2 l_2$$

The values of the intersects give the estimated values of $\ln \delta_1$ and $\ln \delta_2$ respectively, and α and β are the coefficients of k and l respectively in each year.

What are the regression results? The are given below for two successive years for a data set of 205 large listed companies (mainly in the Top 500), being the same companies in each year. (I didn't use more as I had a data problem with the size of the spreadsheet).

OLS Regression Results Year 1

Dep variable	r1	R-squared	0.529
Model	OLS	Adj R Squared	0.525
Method	Least Squares	F-Statistic	113.7
Log-likelihood	-395.81	Prob (F-Statistic)	853e-34
No observations	205	AIC	797.6
Df Residuals	202	BIC	807.6
Df Mode	2		

	Coeff	Std Error	T	P>(t)	(95% Confidence Interval)	
Intercept	1.6881	0.506	3.338	0.001	0.691	2.2685
k1	0.4403	0.055	8.011	0.000	0.332	0.549
l1	0.3850	0.059	6.535	0.000	0.269	0.501

Omnibus	38.801	Durbin Watson	1.757
Prob (omnibus)	0.000	Jacques_Bera (JB)	153.401
Skew	0.655	Prob (JB)	4.89e-34
Kurtosis	7.031	Cond no	56.5

OLS Regression Results Year 2

Dep variable	r2	R-squared	0.415
Model	OLS	Adj R Squared	0.410
Method	Least Squares	F-Statistic	71.75
Log-likelihood	-430.21	Prob (F-Statistic)	286e-24
No observations	205	AIC	866.4
Df Residuals	202	BIC	876.4
Df Mode	2		

	Coeff	Std Error	T	P>(t)	(95% Confidence Interval)	
Intercept	2.3819	0.604	3.946	0.000	1.192	3.572
k2	0.5370	0.065	8.221	0.000	0.408	0.666
l2	0.2195	0.066	3.304	0.001	0.088	0.350

Omnibus	189.216	Durbin Watson	1.898
Prob (Omnibus)	0.000	Jacques_Bira (JB)	7804.215
Skew	3.185	Prob (JB)	0.00
Kurtosis	32.548	Cond no	57.1

Most importantly, it can be seen that at the 95% confidence level, $\ln \delta_1 = \ln \delta_2$. For year 1 the value of $\ln \delta_1$ (the intercept) is 1.6881 with the 95% confidence limits being 0.691 and 2.2685. For year 2 the value of $\ln \delta_2$ (the intercept) is 2.3819 with the 95% confidence limits being 1.192 1nd 3.572. Statistically the limits 1.192 and 2.2685 overlap, Therefore at the 95% confidence level $\ln \delta_1 = \ln \delta_2$. Thus $\ln \delta_1 - \ln \delta_2 = 0$ and so $\ln D_1 - \ln D_2 = 0$.

What about the coefficients of k and l, which are α and β?

The coefficient of k_1 (α_1) is 0.4403 and its 95% confidence limits are 0.332 and 0.549. The coefficient of k_2 (α_2) is 0.5370 and its 95% confidence limits are 0.408 and 0.666.

The 95% confidence limits 0.408 and 0.549 overlap, so at the 95% confidence level $\alpha_1 = \alpha_2$.

The coefficient of l_1 (β_1) is 0.3850 and its 95% confidence limits are 0.269 and 0.501. The coefficient of l_2 (β_2) is 0.2195 and its 95% confidence limits are 0.088 and 0.350.

The 95% confidence limits 0.269 and 0.350 overlap, so at the 95% confidence level $\beta_1 = \beta_2$.

Thus the assumptions used for this model are correct. $\ln D_1 - \ln D_2 = 0$, $\alpha_1 = \alpha_2$ and $\beta_1 = \beta_2$.

In the words of the engineers, it works!

In times of catastrophic change, such as in the period of the Great Financial Crisis, these assumptions would not hold, but in more or less normal times, these formulae work very well, and can be depended upon to calculate the levels of increasing, decreasing and negative returns to scale. And oh yes, as can be seen from the above results, when adding $\alpha + \beta$ in both years, industry does not even closely operate on constant returns to scale.

www.ingramcontent.com/pod-product-compliance
Lightning Source LLC
Chambersburg PA
CBHW081559040426
42444CB00012B/3171